GALILEO

CONQUEROR OF
THE STARS

Nancy Dickmann

Gareth Stevens
PUBLISHING

Please visit our website, **www.garethstevens.com**.
For a free color catalog of all ourhigh-quality books, call toll free 1-800-542-2595 or fax 1-877-542-2596.

Library of Congress Cataloging-in-Publication Data

Dickmann, Nancy.
Galileo: conqueror of the stars / by Nancy Dickmann.
p. cm. – (Superheroes of science)
Includes index.
ISBN 978-1-4824-3137-7 (pbk.)
ISBN 978-1-4824-3140-7 (6 pack)
ISBN 978-1-4824-3138-4 (library binding)
1. Galilei, Galileo, – 1564-1642 – Juvenile literature. 2. Astronomers – Italy – Biography – Juvenile literature.
3. Physicists – Italy – Biography – Juvenile literature. I. Dickmann, Nancy. II. Title.
QB36.G2 D53 2016
520'.92—d23

First Edition

Published in 2016 by
Gareth Stevens Publishing
111 East 14th Street, Suite 349
New York, NY 10003

© 2016 Gareth Stevens Publishing

Produced for Gareth Stevens by Calcium
Editors for Calcium: 3REDCARS
Designers: Paul Myerscough and 3REDCARS

Picture credits: Cover art by Mat Edwards; Dreamstime: Dagadu 4b, Marc-andré Le Tourneux 17t,
Neutronman 26t, Olesiaru 34t, Kenneth Sponsier 35b; NASA: 15c, 26b, 45t, NASA/JPL 29c, NASA/JPL/Space
Science Institute 33c; Shutterstock: AISA/Everett 40b, Vadym Andrushchenko 10c, Anneka 13b, Julia Baturina
20c, Alex James Bramwell 16c, Darios 9t, Oleg Golovnev 43b, Iryna1 22b, Suzane M 38t, Lukiyanova Natalia/
Frenta 14c, Sergey Novikov 7t, Picture 21c, Alexander Raths 18c; Wikimedia Commons: 5t, 23t, 24c, 31c, 36c,
37b, 39tr, 41t, 42c, Artgate Fondazione Cariplo 11t, Eric Gaba/Sting 12c, Michael Reeve 19t, sconosciuto 8b,
Rennett Stowe 28b, University of Michigan Library 25c.

Printed in the United States of America
CPSIA compliance information: Batch #CS15GS: For further information contact Gareth Stevens, New York, New York at 1-800-542-2595.

CONTENTS

Chapter 1

WHO WAS GALILEO?

One night in June 1633, an elderly man sat in a small room, his head in his hands. When morning came, he would have to kneel on his arthritic knees before a roomful of officials—and tell a lie. He was a scientist and astronomer, and he believed firmly that Earth traveled around the sun. However, the Catholic Church said that this could not be true, and the Church was extremely powerful. The old man was faced with a hard choice. He could stand up for what he believed in, defend his lifetime of research, and probably be tortured or executed as a result. Or, he could bow to the pressure and read the statement denying his research—a statement he did not believe in.

The man was Galileo Galilei, one of the most famous scientists of the day. He had a reputation for being confident—even arrogant—in his methods and results.

Whoosh!

Galileo was a pioneer in the study of our solar system. He convinced that the planets t around, or orbit, the sun.

STAR CONTRIBUTION

Super Stargazer

Galileo is famous not just for his theories but also for his inventions. He was not the first person to invent the telescope, but he refined and improved the concept, and was the first person to use one to see objects in the sky in detail.

Galileo believed passionately in a scientist's duty to discover how the world works. He put many accepted theories to the test.

Although he had originally trained as a doctor, his research covered a range of areas, from physics and math to astronomy. Over the course of a long career, he made powerful friends—and powerful enemies.

In Galileo's day, many of the facts about the universe that we take for granted (for example, that the sun is at the center of the solar system) were revolutionary, and even dangerous. Scientists were expected to follow the theories of ancient philosophers, and to solve scientific problems by thinking logically about them, not by conducting experiments. Galileo dared to challenge the established ideas of what was true. He had written books and letters that outline his radical beliefs. Would he pay the price for this?

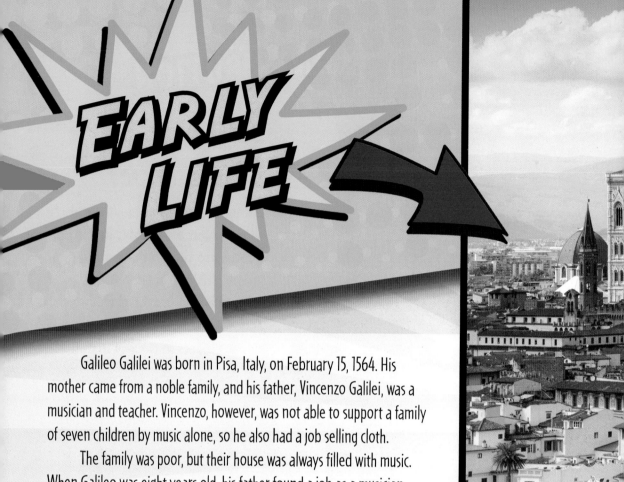

EARLY LIFE

Galileo Galilei was born in Pisa, Italy, on February 15, 1564. His mother came from a noble family, and his father, Vincenzo Galilei, was a musician and teacher. Vincenzo, however, was not able to support a family of seven children by music alone, so he also had a job selling cloth.

The family was poor, but their house was always filled with music. When Galileo was eight years old, his father found a job as a musician with a nobleman in Florence, and two years later the family came to join him. Vincenzo was interested in music theory—the study of the elements of music such as tone, pitch, harmony, and rhythm. He took a scientific approach to studying how to tune instruments, and he passed this on to his son.

Galileo was a very good student. He could read Latin and Greek and showed a curiosity to

SUPERHERO FACT

Expensive Calling

Becoming a monk was not just a religious decision. In Galileo's day, a monk's family was expected to pay a large amount of money to the monastery, and then keep paying to support their son for the rest of his life. Poor families could not afford this.

Wow!

In Galileo's time, Florence was one of the biggest cities in Europe and a center of culture. Many of the beautiful buildings from that time are still standing.

learn about the world. Soon he had reached the limits of what his father could teach him. Money was tight, but the family decided to send him to study at the abbey of Vallombrosa, about 20 miles (30 km) away. In those days, schools run by monks were common. The monks there taught Galileo mathematics, science, and literature, alongside the teachings of the Catholic Church. Galileo thrived in this environment, and at the age of 15 he decided to become a monk. However, Vincenzo was not happy with this idea. He needed his oldest son to choose a profession that would help him support the family. He convinced Galileo to go to university to study to be a doctor instead.

UNSETTLED STUDENT

Galileo entered the University of Pisa in 1581, at the age of 17. Although he was signed up to study medicine, for the first year he had to study Latin, Greek, and Hebrew, and learn about Greek philosophers. Only after that would he start learning about anatomy, math, and other subjects necessary for a doctor. He quickly got bored.

In early 1582, the rulers of Florence arrived in Pisa with their courtiers. One of these men was Ostilio Ricci, the court mathematician. His job was to teach math to the young noblemen of the court. Galileo heard about these lessons and decided to talk his way in. His quick mind and his willingness to think about new ideas caught Ricci's attention, and he continued to teach him, even after the court returned to Florence.

Mathematics at the time involved studying the work of Euclid, Archimedes, and other pioneering ancient Greeks. Galileo found it fascinating, and devoted so much time to studying math

The mathematician Ostilio Ricci taught Galileo the works of Euclid and Archimedes.

City Power!

In Galileo's time, Italy was not a single country. Instead, it was made up of different city-states, each with its own government. The city-state of Tuscany, which included Florence and Pisa, was one of the largest and most powerful.

SUPERHERO FACT

The University of Pisa was founded in 1343 and is one of the oldest universities in the world.

that he neglected his medical studies. He was extremely bright, but also arrogant. He did not try to hide his impatience with the classes in the medical school, and he was scornful of teachers whose ideas he disagreed with.

In the next year or two, Galileo hardly went to class anymore, and he was in danger of failing his exams. Galileo wanted to switch his major from medicine to math, but his father would not agree. He could not afford the tuition fees for another four years, and he did not think that studying math would lead to a good job. At the age of 21, Galileo left university without a degree.

Chapter 2

THE YOUNG SCIENTIST

Without a degree, Galileo found it difficult to get a job. Instead, he gave private math lessons to pay the bills. For the next four years, he continued to teach and study math. Finally, in 1589, he was offered a job at his old university in Pisa, teaching math. It was a low-level position, but it was a start.

At Pisa, Galileo taught not only math, but also several other related subjects, such as astronomy, mechanics, and military engineering. He was fascinated by physics, in particular the study of motion, so he taught his students that as well. When he was not teaching, Galileo kept busy with his own research.

Zoom!

Galileo did careful experiments, rolling balls down a slope over and over and over and taking notes. This was an unusual approach in those days.

One of the most important discoveries Galileo made during this time was his law of uniformly accelerated motion. He was interested in the way that objects fell, and applied his knowledge of math to see if he could predict how fast they would fall. After a lot of

Falling Figures

In Galileo's law of uniformly accelerated motion, an object's speed can be figured out based on the time that passes while it is falling. The calculation involves squaring (multiplying by itself) the amount of time. For example, if a ball falls 3 feet in 1 second (3 x 1 squared = 3 x 1 = 3), it will fall 12 feet in 2 seconds (3 x 2 squared = 3 x 4 = 12), and 27 feet in 3 seconds (3 x 3 squared = 3 x 9 = 27).

Euclid lived in Egypt around 300 BC. His most important book, *Elements*, outlined the principles of geometry.

SUPERHERO STAT

experimentation, he realized that the weight of the falling object made no difference. The speed increased at a regular rate, based on the time it took the object to fall.

Galileo found that this law applied no matter whether an object was dropped from a height or rolled down a slope. He also did a related experiment, involving slopes. He rolled balls down a flat slope, as well as down as an inward-curving, or concave, slope of the same length. The ball rolling on the curved path always reached the end sooner.

TIME-WARP SCIENCE

Galileo's approach was unusual for a scientist of his time. In the sixteenth century, the science and math taught at universities were based on the work of ancient Greek philosophers such as Aristotle and Plato. Aristotle had been one of the greatest scientists of the ancient world. His writings covered a huge range of topics, from botany and chemistry to motion and history. He also founded the study of formal logic. In Galileo's time, most scientists accepted Aristotle's teachings as fact.

Part of the problem was that in those days, the Catholic Church dominated people's thinking. Aristotle's view of the universe was that the heavens were perfect and orderly, but Earth was changeable and imperfect. The Church agreed with this view, since it more or

Aristotle's views on science had a huge influence on scholars, even centuries after his death.

Church Power Play

When Galileo lived, the pope, who was the head of the Catholic Church, had immense power. In some city-states, high-ranking Church officials served as advisers to the rulers—and some popes had even deposed kings. The Church ran many universities, and it could punish people for heresy (going against church teachings) and other crimes.

SUPERHERO FACT

less matched up with what was in the Bible, and disagreeing with it meant disagreeing with Church teachings. This led to scientists not questioning or testing Aristotle's theories—they just had to accept them as true.

Unfortunately, Aristotle had not always been right. In fact, he was wrong about quite a lot. He had relied on reasoning and observation to make sense of the world. He used "inductive reasoning," which means using a small observation to figure out a larger theory, without proving it, for example, saying that since horses live a long time, other similar animals will also live a long time. And in Galileo's time, nearly 2,000 years later, many of Aristotle's theories still had not been tested scientifically.

One of Aristotle's many interests was how animals give birth to young in different ways—for example, laying eggs.

ARISTOTLE CHALLENGE!

It was time to shake things up, and Galileo was the person to do it. "Never assume as true that which requires proof," he said. However, although Galileo may have criticized Aristotle, there were other ancient Greeks he admired. One of them was Archimedes, who was a mathematician as well as an inventor and astronomer. He made incredibly accurate calculations but was also hands-on, building models to test his ideas.

Galileo was determined to follow Archimedes's example and put Aristotle's ideas through rigorous scientific testing. The first example of this was his work on falling objects. Aristotle had said that the speed of a falling object depends on its weight. If this theory were true, a 10-pound (4.5 kg) cannonball would fall twice as fast as a 5-pound (2.25 kg) cannonball, and five times as fast as a 2-pound (0.9 kg) cannonball.

Galileo knew this must be wrong. He wanted to prove it in a dramatic way, so he staged a public demonstration to test Aristotle's theory.

By choosing the most famous building in the city of Pisa, Galileo was guaranteed an audience for his daring demonstration.

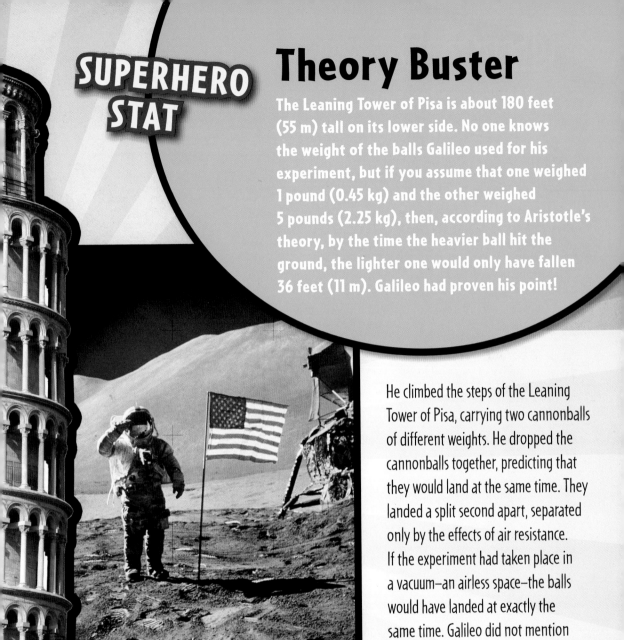

Theory Buster

The Leaning Tower of Pisa is about 180 feet (55 m) tall on its lower side. No one knows the weight of the balls Galileo used for his experiment, but if you assume that one weighed 1 pound (0.45 kg) and the other weighed 5 pounds (2.25 kg), then, according to Aristotle's theory, by the time the heavier ball hit the ground, the lighter one would only have fallen 36 feet (11 m). Galileo had proven his point!

Kpow!

He climbed the steps of the Leaning Tower of Pisa, carrying two cannonballs of different weights. He dropped the cannonballs together, predicting that they would land at the same time. They landed a split second apart, separated only by the effects of air resistance. If the experiment had taken place in a vacuum–an airless space–the balls would have landed at exactly the same time. Galileo did not mention this experiment in any of his notes, and it may not have actually happened. However, it is a great way of illustrating the scientific concept!

In 1971, astronaut David Scott finally proved Galileo right when he dropped a hammer and a feather on the moon. Without air resistance, they landed at exactly the same time.

Chapter 3

MATH, METHOD, AND INVENTION

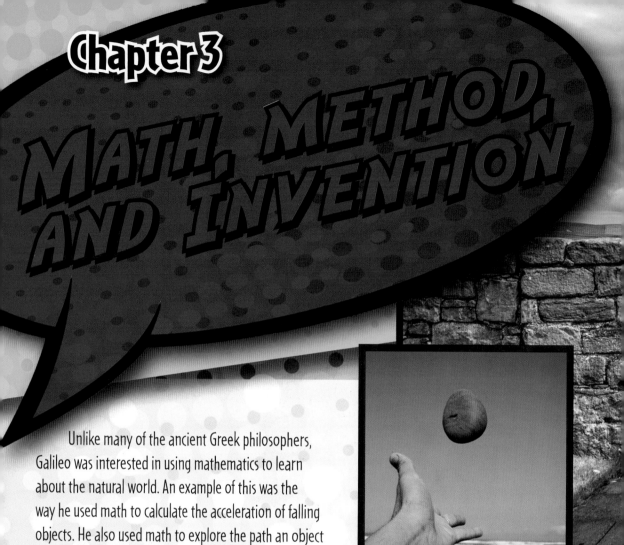

Unlike many of the ancient Greek philosophers, Galileo was interested in using mathematics to learn about the natural world. An example of this was the way he used math to calculate the acceleration of falling objects. He also used math to explore the path an object would take if it were thrown or set into motion another way, like a cannonball shot out of a cannon.

Aristotle had proposed two types of motion—the motion of an object toward its natural place, and motion caused by a force. For example, a stone's natural place is the earth, so when it is dropped, a natural force makes it fall toward the earth. However, what would happen if you threw a stone though the air? If Aristotle's theory were correct, the stone would fall straight toward the ground—but that is not what actually happens. Galileo made a series of experiments and realized that the

What goes up must come down— and it will come down in a curved path called a parabola.

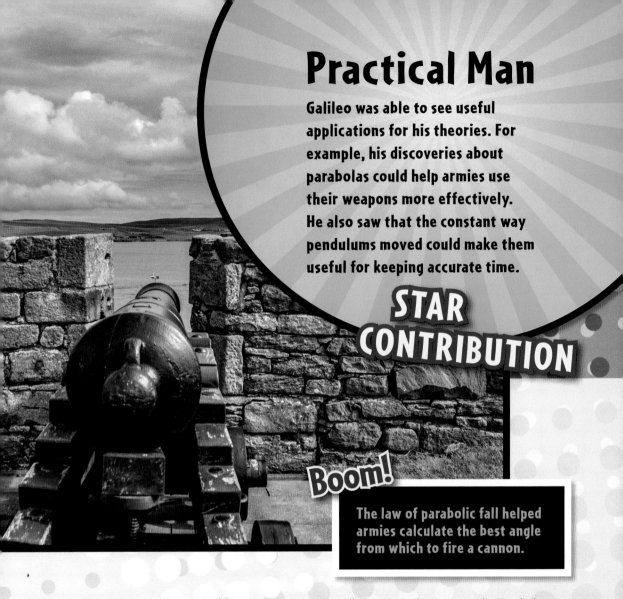

Practical Man

Galileo was able to see useful applications for his theories. For example, his discoveries about parabolas could help armies use their weapons more effectively. He also saw that the constant way pendulums moved could make them useful for keeping accurate time.

STAR CONTRIBUTION

Boom!

The law of parabolic fall helped armies calculate the best angle from which to fire a cannon.

path such an object followed took the shape of a curve, called a parabola. He was able to calculate the length and shape of the curve—called the parabolic fall—and predict where a certain object, such as a cannonball, might land.

Galileo was also interested in pendulums, which were weights that hung from a cord. He had noticed that the time it takes for a pendulum to complete a swing from one side to another is always the same. He experimented and discovered that it does not matter whether a pendulum swings a long distance or a short one, or how heavy the weight at the end is. The length of the string is the only thing that changes the time it takes for the pendulum to swing.

HANDS-ON APPROACH

Galileo was not the first person to challenge Aristotle's view that observation was superior to mathematical calculations and experiments. For example, in the ancient Islamic world, the mathematician and astronomer Ibn al-Haytham conducted scientific experiments, and Roger Bacon, a thirteenth-century English scientist, wrote that people should not blindly accept Aristotle's ideas. However, Galileo took things a step farther, and he helped to develop what we would now call the "scientific method."

The earliest scientists might observe something and then read the works of ancient philosophers and the Bible before trying to reason causes and solutions. Galileo turned that on its head. He believed in starting with observation and careful recording of data, and then making a prediction based on that information, called a hypothesis.

STAR CONTRIBUTION

Spreading the Word

In Galileo's time, nearly all scholars and Church officials wrote in Latin, rather than the language they spoke every day. This meant that scientists in different countries could read each other's work, but it also meant that ordinary people could not. Galileo published some of his work, particularly his later research, in Italian rather than Latin, so that more people could read it.

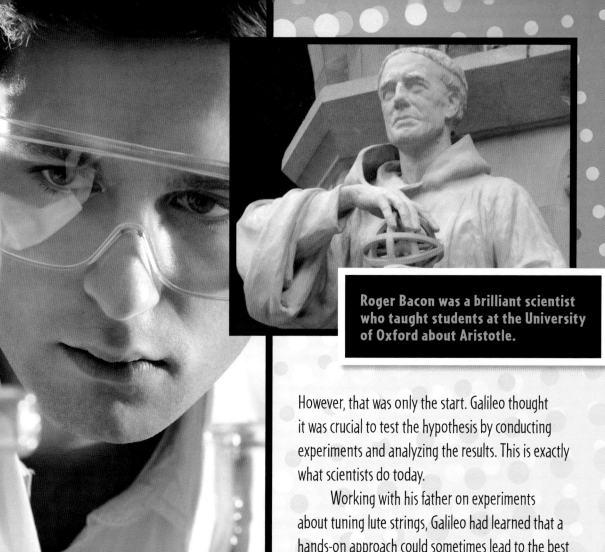

Roger Bacon was a brilliant scientist who taught students at the University of Oxford about Aristotle.

However, that was only the start. Galileo thought it was crucial to test the hypothesis by conducting experiments and analyzing the results. This is exactly what scientists do today.

Working with his father on experiments about tuning lute strings, Galileo had learned that a hands-on approach could sometimes lead to the best results. He applied this to his own scientific work, and often built models to test out his theories. In doing this, he was emulating one of his heroes, Archimedes. Galileo found that he often learned from making the model, as well as from observing it working. This hands-on approach, combined with a desire to find practical applications for his theories, eventually led to Galileo coming up with important inventions.

Zap!

Scientists in laboratories today use the same basic method of experimentation used by Galileo.

MASTER OF INVENTION

One of Galileo's earliest inventions was influenced by his work on pendulums and his medical studies. In Galileo's time, there were no watches or really accurate clocks. Galileo knew that the swing of a pendulum could keep regular time, and so he thought it could help doctors measure the pulse of a patient. He invented a device that became known as the "pulsilogium." It was an adjustable length of cord with a weight at the end. The axle, or shaft, that wound the cord had a dial with figures marked on it. A doctor could set the pulsilogium to a normal pulse rate, and then compare that to a patient's pulse.

Galileo also developed a small balance, called a hydrostatic balance, which could weigh an object in air and in water. Galileo's balance was extremely accurate, and jewelers were able to use it to ensure the purity of their metals.

Boing!

A pendulum's regular swing makes it suitable for clocks, as well as for timing pulse rates.

Money Sense

Although the pulsilogium was popular with doctors, Galileo made no money from it. However, he needed money to help support his family, so he made sure that he kept more control over his later inventions, and even obtained patents for some of them.

SUPERHERO FACT

Galileo also invented a water pump that could be used for pumping water up from reservoirs. The pump worked, but it was a commercial failure.

At one point, Galileo invented an instrument–called a "thermoscope"–that he hoped would measure body temperature. It consisted of a small water-filled vase and a thin glass pipe topped with an empty glass bulb. When the glass bulb got warmer, it made the water rise in the pipe. However, Galileo never got the thermoscope to work effectively.

One of Galileo's most successful inventions was a compass, with two hinged legs, a semicircular scale, and a weighted string. Armies could use the compass to help them aim their cannons more accurately, and to calculate how much gunpowder they should use.

This device is called a Galileo thermometer. The great scientist did not invent it, but it is based on a principle that he discovered.

Chapter 4
THE GREAT ASTRONOMER

After a few years teaching at the University of Pisa, Galileo was offered a job as professor of mathematics at the University of Padua. Padua was part of the city-state of Venice, and Galileo moved there in 1592. The pay was much better than at Pisa, which was a big help. Galileo's father had died the year before, and, as the eldest son, he was now responsible for the rest of his family.

During his time at Padua, Galileo became interested in astronomy. For hundreds of years, scientists had been observing and calculating the movement of objects in the sky, such as the moon and stars. They knew that some objects—the planets—move throughout the year, while the stars stay in a fixed pattern. They also made detailed calculations about the movement of the sun and moon.

Pow!

Galileo was influenced by Nicolaus Copernicus, who was a talented mathematician as well as an astronomer.

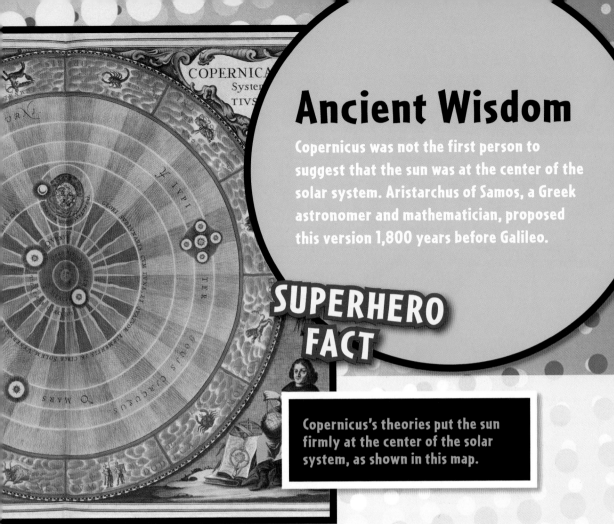

Ancient Wisdom

Copernicus was not the first person to suggest that the sun was at the center of the solar system. Aristarchus of Samos, a Greek astronomer and mathematician, proposed this version 1,800 years before Galileo.

SUPERHERO FACT

Copernicus's theories put the sun firmly at the center of the solar system, as shown in this map.

Until the sixteenth century, most scientists followed Aristotle's teachings about the sky. He thought that planets and other objects in the sky had the shape of perfect spheres, and they traveled in perfectly circular paths. This is close to the truth, although he was wrong about the reasons for it. He was even more wrong, however, about something else—like most other ancient philosophers, Aristotle thought that Earth was at the center of the universe, a theory known as geocentrism.

In 1543, a Polish astronomer named Nicolaus Copernicus published a book, called *On the Revolutions of the Heavenly Spheres*, which offered mathematical proof that Earth orbits the sun, and not the other way around. However, the Catholic Church strongly supported the geocentric version, with Earth at the center. Galileo believed in Copernicus's theories, but it would have been dangerous to state this publicly and openly go against the teachings of the Church.

TELESCOPE TRIUMPHS

In 1609, Galileo heard a rumor about a new invention in the Netherlands–the telescope. Before this instrument, there was no way to make distant objects appear closer or clearer, and astronomers had to make all of their observations with the naked eye. Spectacles and magnifying glasses were available to help people read, but they were only useful for viewing nearby objects. The Dutch telescope could make distant things appear three times larger than actual size.

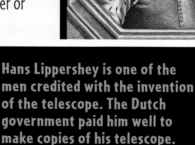

Hans Lippershey is one of the men credited with the invention of the telescope. The Dutch government paid him well to make copies of his telescope.

Galileo had not seen the telescope, but he heard a report that it had been created by a spectacle-maker, using some of his lenses. Based on this information, Galileo was able to figure out how the telescope must work and quickly created his own version. Venice was famous as a center for glassmaking, so he was able to get good lenses made exactly as he wanted them. Galileo's telescope, which was more than twice as powerful as the Dutch version, could magnify things eight times.

Rich Pickings

Galileo's understanding of politics paid off. Thanks to his gift to the doge, the University of Padua offered him a lifetime contract worth 1,000 crowns per year, with an initial bonus of 500 crowns. That was a lot of money, double what he had been paid before.

SUPERHERO STAT

A powerful telescope had many potential uses, especially for the military. For example, a telescope would allow sailors to see ships approaching hours earlier than before. Galileo realized this, and he knew that the doge (the powerful ruler of Venice) would be grateful to a person who could help Venice's military in this way. He was determined to be the one who showed the new invention to the doge. Galileo managed to get a scheduled demonstration of the Dutch telescope postponed until he had perfected his. Then he demonstrated his version to the doge and presented the telescope afterward as a gift.

Galileo wrote this letter to the doge of Venice, offering him the gift of a telescope. The drawings at the bottom right-hand corner show Jupiter's moons.

LOOK TO THE SKY

Many could see the usefulness of a telescope to the military, but Galileo was one of the first people to use one to study the sky. By the fall of 1609, he had managed to make a telescope that could magnify 20 times. One of the first things he used it for was to study the surface of the moon.

Bright and dark patches on the moon are easily visible to the naked eye, but no one knew what they were, or why it was like that. Aristotle's theory was that the moon was close to Earth, so it must have been contaminated by the planet's imperfection. With his telescope, Galileo was able to see even more dark shapes, and he eventually realized that the moon was covered with mountains, valleys, and plains, just like Earth. He concluded

Space probes have given us a better view of the moon's craters than Galileo's telescope was able to.

Shadow Play

Galileo noticed that the light and dark patches on the moon kept changing shape. On Earth, when a source of light moves, the shadows that it causes move too. Galileo thought that the same thing was happening on the moon. He was able to measure these shadows and calculate the height of the moon's mountains.

SUPERHERO FACT

Wow!

Some ancient astronomers believed that the Milky Way was made up of stars, and Galileo's telescope provided evidence for this. Modern radio telescopes have shown us even more about our galaxy.

also that the moon did not create its own light, but reflected light from the sun.

Galileo also used his telescope to study the stars. With the telescope, he was able to see many more stars than anyone thought existed. For example, when he studied the constellation of Orion, he saw more than 80 stars! When he looked at the Milky Way in detail, he could see that it was made up of too many stars to count. There were so many stars, clustered so closely together, that without a telescope it looked like a milky river. However, no matter how much Galileo refined and improved his telescope, he was never able to see any detail on these stars. He realized this meant that they were much, much farther away than anyone had previously thought.

THE GIANT PLANET

Galileo kept working on improvements to his telescope, and in early 1610 he had one that allowed him to see the planet Jupiter as a round disk, a little like how the moon appears. He was surprised to see three bright stars alongside it–two to the east and one to the west. He looked again the next evening and found that the stars had moved. Now all three of them were on the western side of the planet.

The ancient Egyptian astronomer Ptolemy had figured out a plan of the universe in which the sun, moon, and planets orbited Earth. In his version, the stars were fixed, as though stuck to the inside of a giant dome covering the skies. They rotated once every 24 hours, but they did not change position relative to each other. Galileo knew that according to Ptolemy's system, the three stars he saw should now have been on the eastern side

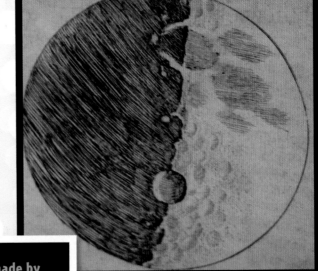

This sketch of the moon, made by Galileo, was included in his book *The Starry Messenger.*

Dynamic Discovery

The implications of Galileo's discovery of Jupiter's moons were huge. No theory of the universe at that time allowed for any body except Earth to have objects orbiting it. Galileo's discovery provided evidence that Copernicus had been right about the sun being the center of the solar system.

STAR CONTRIBUTION

of Jupiter, not the western side. The stars should have stayed in one place, while Jupiter traveled past them from east to west.

What could this mean? Had Ptolemy gotten the orbit of Jupiter backward? Galileo kept watching and soon found a fourth "star," observing that all the stars seemed to be traveling through the skies with Jupiter and were sometimes hidden behind it. He realized at last that they must be moons orbiting Jupiter.

In March 1610, Galileo published a book called *The Starry Messenger.* It contained his observations of the moon and stars, as well as the moons of Jupiter. He included charts of constellations, or groups of stars, which showed stars not seen with the naked eye.

Zoom!

One of the "stars" that Galileo saw was Ganymede, the largest moon in the solar system. It is bigger than the planet Mercury, but because it orbits Jupiter and not the sun, it cannot be called a planet.

Chapter 5

FAME AND FORTUNE

The publication of *The Starry Messenger* caused quite a stir across Europe. It sold out quickly, and suddenly everyone wanted a telescope to see these wonders of the skies for themselves. Galileo had opened the door to a whole new world that no one knew existed. People wrote poems about Galileo, and painters used the charts to put accurate constellations in their paintings.

However, not all reaction to the book was positive. Galileo's observations and theories supported Copernicus's view of the universe, not the Church's. There was also the problem that no one else had a telescope as powerful as Galileo's and so could not duplicate his results. People had to take his word for it, and many were unwilling to do that. However, in the fall of 1610, a number of other astronomers were able to observe the moons of Jupiter through improved telescopes and confirm Galileo's findings.

Galileo was a respected part of the faculty at Padua, but he missed Florence. A few years earlier, one of his students had been Cosimo de' Medici, part of the powerful

Grand Duke Cosimo II de' Me
an important supporter and
of Galileo. His family, the Me
had started off as powerful
bankers in Florence and the
on to rule Tuscany for centu

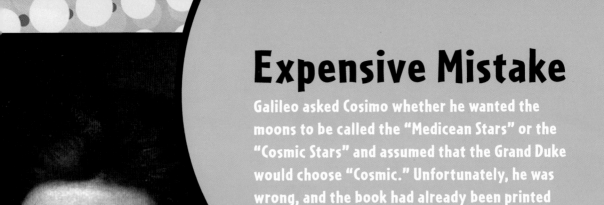

Expensive Mistake

Galileo asked Cosimo whether he wanted the moons to be called the "Medicean Stars" or the "Cosmic Stars" and assumed that the Grand Duke would choose "Cosmic." Unfortunately, he was wrong, and the book had already been printed with the term "Cosmic." A strip of paper with the correct name had to be glued into each copy!

SUPERHERO FACT

Medici family that ruled the Grand Duchy of Tuscany, based around Florence. When *The Starry Messenger* was published, Cosimo had recently become the Grand Duke, and Galileo wanted to get on his good side. He dedicated the book to him, and in it he gave the name "Medicean Stars" to the moons of Jupiter.

Galileo's plan worked, and Cosimo offered him a job as his Chief Mathematician. This meant moving back to Florence, where he would receive the same salary as he was getting in Padua. Even better, he did not have to teach and could devote all his time to research.

PLANET SHAPESHIFTER

Galileo was glad to be back in Florence, where he became rich and well respected. He continued to observe the sky, focusing on the planet Saturn first. At the time, people believed Saturn to be the farthest planet from Earth, and they assumed it was a perfect sphere, like everything else in the heavens. Seen through Galileo's telescope, however, Saturn looked like it had ears. What could be causing this strange shape?

Because of what he had learned about Jupiter, Galileo's first thought was that there were two moons orbiting close to Saturn, although he could not see a gap between the "moons" and the planet. In 1612, the "moons" seemed to disappear, and then they reappeared in 1613. Galileo was mystified, and he never published a theory about them.

Galileo's telescope was not powerful enough to allow him to see Saturn's rings clearly. With the help of visiting spacecraft such as Cassini, which took this photograph, astronomers can now see fine detail in Saturn's rings.

He also spent a lot of time observing Venus, and made a groundbreaking discovery. Our moon appears to change shape because only the side of it facing the sun is lit, and we see different amounts of the lit part, depending on where the moon is in its orbit of Earth.

Finding the Ring

Galileo never did figure out what gave Saturn its odd shape. It was nearly 50 years later that a Dutch astronomer, Christiaan Huygens, proposed the idea that Saturn was surrounded by a ring.

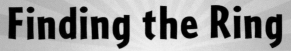

One of the criticisms of Copernicus's theory was that if the sun was really at the center of the universe, then the planets Mercury and Venus should have phases (that is, appear to change shape) like the moon does. And up until then, anyone could see that they did not.

However, no one had ever had a telescope as powerful as Galileo's before. By making careful observations of Venus over a period of three months, he watched it change from a round disk down to a thin crescent, and then back again. This proved once and for all that Ptolemy had been wrong about planets orbiting Earth.

SUNSPOT SENSATION

Another of Galileo's areas of research would call into question even more Church teachings. Toward the end of 1610, he had first observed what looked like spots on the sun. It is dangerous to look directly at the sun, especially through a telescope, but Galileo used his to project an image of the sun onto paper, which he could then trace. After careful observation, he was ready to go public with his theories.

Phew!

Sunspots had been seen in ancient times, and by some medieval astronomers. However, many assumed that they were planets passing in front of the sun.

Galileo had noticed that a sunspot took about two weeks to travel across the sun. However, the sunspot appeared to move more slowly when it was near the edges of the sun. He realized that this was the effect of foreshortening. Near the edge, the spot is moving toward you as it circles the sun, but you cannot see this 3-D effect from Earth, so it just looks like it is traveling slowly across the face of the sun. This could only happen if the spots were on, or only just above, the surface of the sun.

Hot Spots!

We now know that sunspots are caused by disturbances in the sun's magnetic field. They appear dark because they are cooler than the areas surrounding them, but they are still incredibly hot—around 7,200 °F (4,000 °C)! Most sunspots are anywhere from 1,500 miles (2,500 km) to 31,000 miles (50,000 km) in diameter. Sunspots come and go in an irregular cycle that lasts about 11 years.

SUPERHERO STAT

This may seem like an obvious conclusion, but it flew in the face of what was believed about the sun. According to the Catholic Church—and to Aristotle—the sun was perfect. The Bible said that God had created the sun to give light to the world, so it was unthinkable that there could be blemishes on it. They must be clouds, or planets, many scientists said—even specks of something inside Galileo's telescope. Galileo knew he was right, and he put his theories in writing—a dangerous move.

A planet transiting, or passing across, the sun (shown here) appears to travel at a consistent speed, unlike sunspots.

Chapter 6

GALILEO AND THE CHURCH

By the end of 1610, Galileo was famous and respected by his peers, and he had powerful friends, such as Grand Duke Cosimo. He was also supremely confident in his abilities as a scientist. He must have felt he was in a strong position, or he would not have published research that contradicted the Church's teachings. In the seventeenth century, the penalties for getting on the wrong side of the Church could be harsh.

In those days, the Church had the authority to put people on trial for religious crimes. An organization called the Inquisition was a part of the Church's judicial system. Its main goals were to punish heresy (disagreeing with church teachings) and to stamp out the various groups that broke off from the main Church. A person who was found guilty of heresy could be sentenced to death—often by being burned at the stake. The Inquisition was clear that the point of these drastic sentences was to frighten others into toeing the line.

Galileo demonstrated his telescope to Pope Paul V, who was delighted with it. However, the pope later cautioned him about defending Copernicus's ideas.

Living Dangerously

When Galileo was at the University of Padua, he was in the city-state of Venice, where the pope and the Catholic Church had less influence than elsewhere. No one was ever prosecuted for heresy in Venice. In Tuscany, however, where Galileo had moved, the Church had more power. Florence was a more dangerous place to be for someone, like Galileo, who was going against Church teachings.

SUPERHERO FACT

Copernicus only published his theories just before he died, possibly because he was worried about the reaction from the Inquisition. In 1616, decades after his death, the Inquisition ruled that his theory stating that the sun was at the center of the universe was "foolish and absurd" as well as heretical. Copernicus's groundbreaking work was placed on a list of forbidden books, where it stayed until 1758.

Teachings or writings that criticized the Catholic Church or its views were harshly punished. The German priest Martin Luther was forced to go into hiding after starting the process that would split the Protestant Church from the Catholic Church.

GETTING INTO TROUBLE

If the Inquisition received an accusation of heresy against someone, it had to investigate it. Unfortunately, Galileo was good at making enemies. He had a habit of ridiculing people whose ideas he disagreed agree with, even fellow scientists, and his success at the court of Tuscany made others jealous. Also, leaders of the Catholic Church felt threatened by his publication of scientific theories that seemed to contradict the Bible.

In 1611, Galileo had visited Rome and demonstrated his telescope to Pope Paul V, and was treated like a celebrity. Four years later he went back in very different circumstances–to defend himself against an accusation of heresy.

STAR CONTRIBUTION

Big Mistake

Galileo was a great scientist, but he was not always right. He spent time studying tides, and eventually decided they were the result of the motion of Earth on its axis, as well as its movement around the sun. He disagreed with the astronomer Johannes Kepler, who proposed that the "attractive force of the moon" caused tides. Kepler was right about the moon, and Galileo mistakenly mocked him.

Galileo shared some of his discoveries with Johannes Kepler, a German astronomer who agreed with many of this theories.

Whoosh!

We now know that the pull of the sun and the moon causes tides. Isaac Newton's theories of gravity, published about 70 years after Kepler's ideas, gave the explanation.

The charges were dropped, but he was given a formal warning against teaching, defending, or even discussing Copernicus's theories. However, he could continue his research, as long as he treated the theory of heliocentrism—which stated that the sun is at the center of the solar system—as unproven.

Galileo had a short temper, and when a Jesuit mathematician published an article that claimed to prove Copernicus wrong, it turned into a war of words between the two men. Galileo ended up writing a book, *The Assayer*. It did not mention Copernicus directly, but it outlined Galileo's theory of science in bold terms. The new pope, Urban VIII, loved the book, making Galileo think that he was now safe from the Inquisition. He began work on his next book, *Dialogue Concerning the Two Chief World Systems*, which compared the theories of Aristotle and Copernicus.

PAYING THE PRICE

Galileo's book *Dialogue Concerning the Two Chief World Systems* took the form of a discussion between three friends, comparing the views of Copernicus and Ptolemy on the solar system. However, the character who spoke up for Aristotle was made to look foolish, and some claimed that he was based on the pope. The book was approved for publication by a Church official in Florence, but then banned by the Inquisition. Galileo was ordered to Rome to answer charges of heresy.

Galileo arrived in Rome in February 1633, after a long and difficult journey. He was nearly 70 years old and not in good health. For two months, he remained under arrest at the Tuscan embassy, waiting for his trial to begin. Between April and June, he appeared at four different hearings.

Galileo's defense was that his book did not argue that Copernicus's theory was correct, rather merely discussed it as a theory. He offered to write an extra chapter to show that Copernicus had been wrong, but the Inquisition believed he was telling them what he thought they wanted to hear—which was probably correct.

Kpow!

At his trial, Galileo was questioned very closely, as the prosecutors tried to determine if he really believed Copernicus's theories.

Lucky Escape

Galileo was lucky to escape with his life. About 30 years earlier, a friar named Giordano Bruno was burned at the stake for a variety of heresies, including a belief that Earth traveled around the sun, and that the universe was infinite.

Pope Urban VIII started as a supporter of Galileo, but he was responsible for putting him on trial.

They wanted to examine Galileo's intentions in writing the book—had he intended for Copernicus's theory to appear more plausible than the other ideas? The Inquisition made it clear that they could use any method, including torture, to get their answers.

Faced with torture and possible execution, Galileo backed down. He stated that he did not believe in Copernicus's version of the solar system, and never had. He read out a confession that the Church officials wrote for him. He was sentenced to remain in prison for an indefinite time.

FINAL YEARS AND DEATH

Although he had been convicted of heresy, Galileo still had powerful friends. Thanks to their influence, he was transferred from the jail at the Vatican, the pope's stronghold, to the relative comfort of the Tuscan embassy. Shortly afterward, Cardinal Piccolomini, the archbishop of Siena and a former student of Galileo's, persuaded the authorities to let Galileo serve out his sentence under his roof.

The stress of the trial had taken a toll on Galileo. He was already in poor health, and the conviction shattered his confidence. The archbishop did his best to raise his spirits. He ordered lenses with which to make a telescope, and the two of them studied the sky together. Piccolomini suggested that Galileo

In his later years Galileo was troubled by poor health, and he had a team of assistants to help him experiment and write.

Keeping the Faith

According to legend, after confessing to the inquisitors, Galileo muttered "Eppur si muove" under his breath, which means "And yet it moves." He was referring to Earth and his firm belief—regardless of what he had confessed under pressure—that it moved around the sun. There is no firm evidence that he actually said these words, but they have become a rallying cry for scientists everywhere.

STAR CONTRIBUTION

go back to his study of the laws of motion, which were less likely to annoy the Church. By the end of 1633, Galileo was allowed to go back to his villa outside Florence, where he remained under house arrest for the rest of his life.

The Inquisition banned his books but did not have the power to enforce this outside Italy. Galileo arranged for *Dialogue Concerning the Two Chief World Systems* to be smuggled out and published elsewhere. His visitors were restricted, but he was allowed to write and receive letters from scientists all over Europe.

By the end of 1637, Galileo had gone blind, but his busy mind kept working on physics, motion, pendulums, and longitude. In late 1641, however, he became seriously sick and died in January of the following year. He was 77 years old.

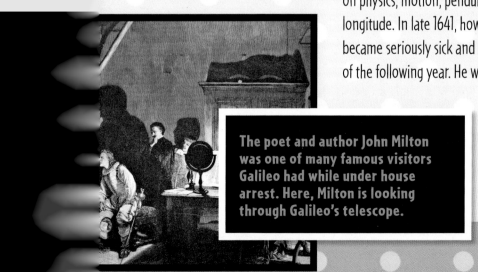

The poet and author John Milton was one of many famous visitors Galileo had while under house arrest. Here, Milton is looking through Galileo's telescope.

GALILEO'S LEGACY

Regardless of his confession, there is no doubt that
Galileo believed firmly in the Copernican theory until the
day he died. Some critics have said he was a coward to
confess, and that he should have stood up for his beliefs,
no matter what the consequences were. However, Galileo
was a practical person. If he had not confessed, there was
a good chance he would have been executed. So he did
confess, in the hope he would be left free to continue
his research. In the end, Galileo made several important
scientific discoveries while under house arrest.

Galileo's impact on the scientific world was huge. Albert Einstein called him "the father of
modern physics–indeed of modern science altogether." His careful methods and analytical approach,
and his willingness to question established beliefs, have become the template for scientists ever since.
Before Galileo, most scientists based their work on the writings of past scientists. He was one of the
first to use experiments as a way of investigating the world.

Even the Catholic Church eventually admitted that Galileo had been right. In 1758, the Church
lifted its ban on books supporting heliocentrism, although Galileo's *Dialogue* and Copernicus's

Star Scientist

Galileo is mainly remembered for his work in astronomy, but his research covered a wide range of topics, including motion, medicine, and math. In particular, his work on physics and motion was ahead of its time. Many of Galileo's findings can still be found in textbooks today.

Whiz!

The Galileo mission was launched in 1989 and its spacecraft became the first to orbit Jupiter.

On the Revolutions of the Heavenly Spheres remained banned until 1835. In 1992, Pope John Paul II issued a statement expressing regret at how Galileo had been treated by the Church.

Since his death, Galileo has been the subject of many books, plays, and paintings. There are statues, coins, and stamps honoring him, and the four largest moons of Jupiter, which he called the "Medicean Stars," are now called the Galilean moons. And he has even been into space! The *Juno* spacecraft, which launched in 2011, carries a tiny, specially made LEGO model of Galileo. This will get to orbit Jupiter, the planet Galileo studied so closely through his telescope, in 2016.

Glossary

abbey a religious building where monks live and work

acceleration the act of an object increasing its speed

air resistance the friction caused when an object moves through the air, which can slow down falling objects

anatomy the study of the human body and how it works

applications practical ways of putting a theory into use

astronomy the study of the sun, moon, planets, stars, and everything else in the universe

city-states self-governing states made up of a city and the surrounding territory

constellation a group of stars that appear to make a shape or pattern when seen from Earth

court the palace where a ruler, such as king or emperor, lives, and the people who make up his entourage

courtiers the people who are part of a ruler's court

doge the elected leader of Venice and some other Italian city-states during the time of Galileo

execute to put to death as punishment for a crime

foreshortening a distortion of the lines of a visual image

geocentrism the theory that states that Earth is at the center of the solar system or the universe

heliocentrism the theory that states that the sun is at the center of the solar system

heresy a religious belief that goes against the established teachings of the Church

hypothesis a prediction that can be tested scientifically

Inquisition an agency of the Catholic Church that investigated heresy

magnetic field the space around a magnet or other object, such as the sun, where a magnetic force is active

mechanics the branch of mathematics that deals with motion and the forces that produce motion

monks men who have joined together in a religious community and taken vows to live a simple, prayerful life

nobleman a man of high rank or title

orbit to travel around another object in a regular path, such as how the moon orbits Earth

pendulum a weight hung on a long cord, which swings back and forth

philosophers people who study the nature of life, truth, knowledge, and other important subjects

pope the leader of the Catholic Church

scientific method a process used by scientists to make new discoveries, whereby they develop theories that are then tested by experiments

sunspot one of the dark patches that are sometimes seen on the surface of the sun

telescope a tool used for making faraway objects appear bigger

theories ideas about the reason for something, which can be tested by the scientific method

tides the changes in the height of the surface of an ocean or other body of water. Tides are caused by the pull of the moon and the sun

torture causing great physical pain to a person, in order to find out secrets or force a confession

transit to pass across the disk of the sun. Transits of Mercury and Venus can be observed from Earth

vacuum an enclosed space that contains no matter, not even air

For More Information

Books

Andronik, Catherine M. *Copernicus: Founder of Modern Astronomy* (Great Minds of Science). Berkeley Heights, NJ: Enslow Publishers, 2006.

Demuth, Patricia Brennan. *Who Was Galileo?* New York, NY: Grosset & Dunlap, 2015.

Hightower, Paul W. *Galileo: Genius Astronomer* (Genius Scientists and Their Genius Ideas). Berkeley Heights, NJ: Enslow Publishers, 2015.

Miller, Ron. *Recentering the Universe: The Radical Theories of Copernicus, Kepler, Galileo, and Newton*. Minneapolis, MN: Lerner Publishing Group, 2013.

Steele, Philip. *Galileo: The Genius Who Charted the Universe* (National Geographic World History Biographies). Washington, DC: National Geographic Children's Books, 2008.

Websites

Find all about Galileo's life and work, including photographs and timelines, from The Galileo Project, at: **http://galileo.rice.edu**

For an explanation of the scientific method that Galileo used—and scientists today use—see this video, at: **www.youtube.com/watch?v=9kf51FpBuXQ**

Find ten interesting facts about Galileo, at: **http://blog.oup.com/2013/08/10-facts-galileo**

Learn about the spacecraft named after Galileo on NASA's website, at: **http://solarsystem.nasa.gov/missions/profile.cfm?MCode=Galileo**

Discover more about geocentrism and heliocentrism, at: **www.universetoday.com/36487/difference-between-geocentric-and-heliocentric**

Index